A First-Start Easy Reader

This easy reader contains only 57 different words,
repeated often to help the young reader develop
word recognition and interest in reading.

Basic word list for *Mike's New Bike*

a	her	will
is	man	Mike
his	this	Mike's
it	old	bike
to	new	grow
and	when	grew
but	got	rides
in	was	knees
the	big	arms
I	with	looks
too	now	need
my	are	needs
am	way	wants
do	like	want
you	says	going
for	shop	ride
he	can	right
she	just	sister
be	what	little

Mike's New Bike

Written by Rose Greydanus

Illustrated by Deborah Sims

Troll Associates

This is Mike.

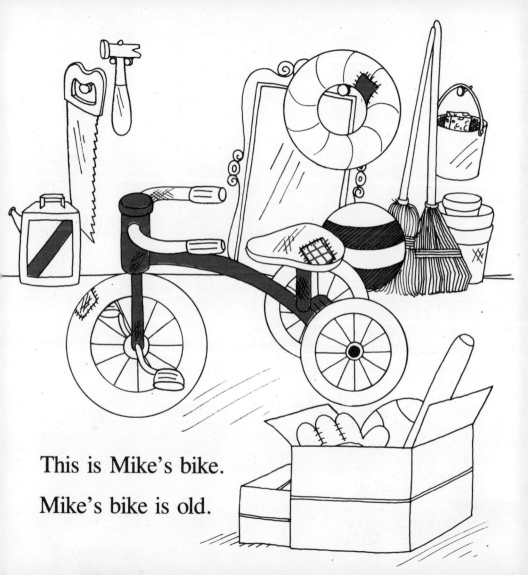

This is Mike's bike.

Mike's bike is old.

When Mike got his bike,

it was too big.

And Mike was too little.

But Mike grew and grew.

Now, Mike's bike is too little.

And Mike is too big.

When Mike rides his bike,
his knees are in the way.

His arms are in the way.

Mike is going to the bike shop.

"I need a new bike," says Mike.

"My old bike is too little.

And I am too big."

"Do you like this bike, Mike?"

says the man.

"Can you ride this bike, Mike?"

"This bike is just right," says Mike.

"I am just right for this bike."

"What will you do with the old bike?"

says the man.

"My sister can ride my old bike,"
says Mike.

"My sister is little.

But she will grow and grow."

"My bike will be just right for her."